Author: Daisy Dewi
ISBN HARDBACK: 978-9916-89-226-8
ISBN PAPERBACK: 978-9916-89-227-5
ISBN EBOOK: 978-9916-89-228-2

The Ties That Bind

Through laughter shared and whispers soft,
We weave our dreams and lift them aloft.
With every challenge, hand in hand,
The ties we hold, forever stand.

In sunset's glow, our stories run,
Together, shining like the sun.
With every heartbeat, closer we find,
The bonds unbroken, the ties that bind.

Echoes Across the Ages

In twilight's glow, old tales are spun,
Voices of the past, like rivers, run.
They whisper softly, secrets to share,
Echoes of love that linger in air.

Through time they travel, through joy and tears,
Carving memories across the years.
Each heartbeat hums with stories untold,
For in our hearts, their warmth we hold.

Waves of Shared Memories

Like ocean's tide that flows and ebbs,
Our moments merge in gentle webs.
Each laugh, each tear, a grain of sand,
Together we rise, together we stand.

In the rhythm of waves, our memories dance,
Caught in the light, an endless romance.
With every crest, our spirits align,
In the vast sea of time, your heart meets mine.

Symphony of Us

In every note, a story we weave,
A melody built on love we believe.
Harmonies blend, our voices unite,
Creating a song that shines so bright.

Through crescendos bold and whispers sweet,
Life plays a tune, a rhythmic beat.
In the music of time, forever we'll tread,
In this symphony of love, we are led.

A Journey Without End

We set forth on paths unknown,
With dreams to guide our way.
Stars above like candles,
Whispering night and day.

Mountains high and rivers wide,
Each bend a tale to tell.
Through valleys deep, we walk with pride,
In nature's gentle spell.

Winds of change, they call our names,
In every step we find.
The echoes of our laughter,
Forever intertwined.

With each sunrise, hope is born,
In the fabric of the sky.
We forge ahead together,
With hearts that dare to fly.

Though the roads may twist and turn,
And shadows may descend,
In this quest, we'll never yearn,
For it's a journey without end.

The Language of Us

In quiet moments shared,
A glance speaks more than words.
Our hearts converse in whispers,
Like songs sung by the birds.

Each smile a gentle promise,
In the fabric of our days.
We dance through life's sweet seasons,
In each other's warm gaze.

Through laughter and through sorrow,
We build a bridge of trust.
Together we find solace,
In the bond that is a must.

The silences between us,
Are filled with love's embrace.
In this language of our hearts,
We find our perfect place.

United in our journey,
With every step we take.
This language that we cherish,
Is the love we cultivate.

Spirals of Love

Like ancient seashells winding,
Our love takes shape and form.
In spirals ever-growing,
Through the calm and through the storm.

Round and round, we journey,
Finding new paths to explore.
In layers soft and tender,
We discover so much more.

Moments stitched together,
With threads of joy and pain.
Where hearts entwined in wonder,
Dance beneath the rain.

Each twist holds a promise,
In the rhythm of our days.
As we spiral ever closer,
Through love's warm, embracing ways.

In this sacred spiraling,
We learn what love can be.
For in every sweet circle,
Is a deeper mystery.

Unraveled Threads of Affection

In the tapestry of moments,
Our lives begin to weave.
Each thread a simple story,
Of dreams we believe.

Colors blend and brighten,
As memories take flight.
In the softness of affection,
We find our way to light.

Some threads may fray and falter,
Yet beauty still remains.
For unraveling can lead us,
To a new set of gains.

With every twist and turn,
We gather strength anew.
In the love we share together,
Our hearts begin to grew.

So let the threads unravel,
For in this playful dance,
We stitch a life of meaning,
In every fleeting chance.

A Symphony of Souls

In the hush of twilight's glow,
Soft whispers dance on winds that flow.
Hearts entwined in harmony,
A song of dreams that set us free.

Each note a story, every beat,
A rhythm where our spirits meet.
Bound by faith and love's embrace,
Together we illuminate this space.

With every chord, a journey shared,
In this symphony, we are paired.
The echoes linger, sweet and true,
A melody crafted just for two.

So let the world fade far away,
In perfect harmony, we'll stay.
With every breath, a harmonized role,
Together we play, a symphony of souls.

Infinite Reflections of Us

In mirrors deep, we find our grace,
Infinite reflections that time can't erase.
Fractals of love in each gazing stare,
A universe captured in moments we share.

Like ripples that dance on still waters,
Every glance enchants and never falters.
A tapestry woven with colors so bright,
Infinite hues in the soft evening light.

Through valleys dark and mountains tall,
We journey together, answering the call.
In shadows cast, our spirits align,
Infinite reflections, your heart in mine.

Every heartbeat, a mark of the past,
An endless echo in memories cast.
With each turn of fate, our stories unfurl,
In the tapestry of life, we twirl and swirl.

In every shimmer, your eyes are a guide,
Leading me forward, nowhere to hide.
Through the corridors of space and time,
Infinite reflections, our love is sublime.

Together in the Echo

In stillness, we hear the echo awake,
A resonance of dreams that never break.
Voices of the past weave through our minds,
Together we dance where fate unwinds.

Every whisper carries a heartbeat's song,
In the fields of time, we both belong.
With laughter that lingers, joy that flows,
In togetherness, our love only grows.

The world may falter, but we stand strong,
In the echoes, we know we belong.
Arm in arm, through storms we tread,
Together in echoes, no words left unsaid.

The serenade of life plays on repeat,
Filling the silence with memories sweet.
In this rhythm, our spirits entwine,
Together in echoes, forever we shine.

Let each moment be a cherished line,
In the book of us, the greatest design.
As echoes linger, time bends and sways,
Together we write our endless days.

Merging Horizons

The sun dips low, horizons blend,
Where time and space gracefully mend.
In twilight's arms, we find our way,
Merging horizons at the close of day.

Colors collide in a soft embrace,
As shadows dance, each finds its place.
In the twilight glow, dreams ignite,
As day surrenders to the night.

With every step, we draw so near,
In whispered vows, our love is clear.
Two souls entwined, a joyous dance,
Merging horizons, a serendipitous chance.

As stars awaken in the canvas above,
We craft our dreams in the name of love.
Together we paint from dusk till dawn,
Merging horizons, our hearts drawn.

In this embrace, the world fades away,
As we journey on, come what may.
For in each moment, together we soar,
Merging horizons, forevermore.

Infinity in Your Eyes

In the depths of your gaze, I see,
A universe vast, wild, and free.
Stars that dance, a cosmic show,
A boundless love that continues to grow.

Whispers of dreams in twilight's glow,
Eternal echoes that gently flow.
Your laughter, a melody soft and bright,
Guides me through the darkest night.

Every glance, a promise made,
In your presence, I am not afraid.
With you, time seems to cease,
A serene moment, a beautiful peace.

Together we dive into the unknown,
Finding treasures in places unshown.
The journey unfolds with each shared breath,
In the infinity of love, we conquer death.

In your eyes, I find my home,
In this vast cosmos, we freely roam.
Hand in hand, we chase the skies,
Forever lost in infinity's ties.

Harmonies of Togetherness

In the morning light, we rise,
Together, we weave the sweetest ties.
With every note, our hearts align,
Creating rhythms, pure and divine.

Side by side, we face the day,
With laughter's song, we find our way.
In the garden of hope, we bloom,
Our love, a symphony that fills the room.

Through trials and joys, we stay near,
In the melodies of love, there's no fear.
Creating a chorus, rich and bright,
Our hearts entwined, an endless flight.

With every heartbeat, a soft refrain,
Together, we dance through joy and pain.
We paint the air with colors bold,
In the harmonies of togetherness, we are gold.

Night falls gently, stars take their place,
In the silence, we find our grace.
Wrapped in sound, we softly sigh,
Together forever, you and I.

Paths Intertwined

Two souls walking, side by side,
In the tapestry of life, we confide.
With every step, our stories blend,
A journey together that will never end.

Through valleys low and mountains high,
With hands held tight, we touch the sky.
In every laughter, every tear,
We find our strength, we conquer fear.

Crossroads come and choices loom,
Yet in your light, I find my room.
Paths intertwined, an endless road,
A shared adventure, a sacred code.

In the whispers of a soft breeze,
In every moment, our hearts freeze.
We create memories, vivid and bright,
Two souls forever, lost in light.

Through storms we weather, and sunlit days,
Our love's a compass that always stays.
On this path, we will thrive,
Together forever, we are alive.

The Infinite Canvas of Love

On a canvas stretched wide and bright,
We paint our dreams in hues of light.
Each brushstroke, a story untold,
In the colors of love, our hearts unfold.

From gentle whispers to joyous screams,
We capture moments in vivid dreams.
With every shade, we build our space,
An infinite pattern, an endless grace.

Together we craft with heart and soul,
In the gallery of life, we are whole.
Each color mixed, each shadow cast,
A masterpiece growing, forever vast.

In the chaos of life, we create our art,
In every finish, a brand new start.
With passion and truth, our spirits soar,
On this canvas of love, we explore.

With every heartbeat, we define,
The endless strokes of love, divine.
Together we stand, hand in hand,
On the infinite canvas, forever we'll land.

Timeless Embrace in Space

In the void where stars ignite,
We drift together, hearts in flight.
Galaxies whisper ancient tales,
Of love that soars, never pales.

Cosmic waves, they pull us near,
Through nebulae, we share no fear.
With every heartbeat, light doth trace,
A timeless dance, our sacred space.

Orbiting dreams, we blaze anew,
In every echo, I find you.
Gravity bends in our embrace,
Lost forever in this place.

Light years melt, as moments blend,
With every glance, our souls transcend.
The universe sings our refrain,
Together always, love's domain.

Stars collide and constellate,
In cosmic love, we our fates.
Eternity holds our names in grace,
In this timeless, boundless space.

Threads of Togetherness

In the tapestry of our days,
We weave our dreams in countless ways.
Each thread a moment, bright and true,
Stitched with love, a bond we brew.

Courage flows through every seam,
In laughter shared, we find our dream.
Through tears and joy, we gently thread,
A quilt of warmth beneath our bed.

Hands intertwined, we share the light,
Through darkest hours, we hold on tight.
The fabric of life so richly spun,
In every heartbeat, we are one.

As seasons change, we rise and fall,
Together bound, we conquer all.
The golden threads that fate has spun,
Will guide us forth until we're done.

With every stitch, a story told,
Of love enduring, fierce and bold.
In unity, our spirits soar,
Together always, evermore.

Love's Infinite Loop

In every glance, a spark ignites,
A loop of hope, in day and night.
With every breath, we find a way,
To dance in love, come what may.

Through time's embrace, we intertwine,
In laughter shared, our souls align.
Circles endless, turning fast,
In love's sweet hold, we find our past.

Whispers soft, the echoes sing,
In this loop, the joy you bring.
Round and round, we journey deep,
In love's embrace, our hearts will leap.

We'll face the storms, we'll brave the night,
With every challenge, we take flight.
Forever bound, our spirits rise,
In love's embrace, we find the skies.

In every dawn, a promise made,
In loops of love, we will not fade.
An endless dance, where we belong,
In this infinite loop, love's song.

Whispered Promises Through Time

In twilight's glow, our voices blend,
Whispered promises that never end.
Through ages vast, our hearts will flow,
Wherever time takes us, love will grow.

Every heartbeat, a vow we share,
In dreams we weave, we linger there.
With gentle touches, we mark the days,
In whispered truths, our love conveys.

As seasons shift, and years unfold,
Our stories told, in warmth, so bold.
Time may test, but we stand firm,
In whispered promises, love's eternal term.

In starlit nights, where secrets creep,
We hold the past, while futures leap.
Each promise whispered, soft and clear,
In every breath, I draw you near.

Through time's embrace, our spirits rise,
In every whisper, a sweet disguise.
An endless journey, love defines,
In whispered promises, through all times.

Reflections in a Shared Mirror

In the glass, we find our truth,
Each smile shared, a bridge from youth.
Echoes dance in silent night,
Truths unveiled in soft moonlight.

Every glance, a story told,
In every wrinkle, memories hold.
We cast our dreams into the air,
In this mirror, we both share.

Through the haze of joy and pain,
We find peace beneath the rain.
Your eyes, a map of distant stars,
Leading me through life's avatars.

Moments frozen, time stands still,
Within each glance, a graceful thrill.
As we grow, our spirits mingle,
In this bond, our hearts do tingle.

Together we craft a precious tale,
In reflections, we will never pale.
With every laugh, and every sigh,
In this shared mirror, you and I.

Boundless Horizons of Us

Chasing sunsets, hand in hand,
Across the shore, we carve our stand.
With every wave that kisses sand,
Together, we dream, together, we plan.

The sky unfolds a canvas bright,
In colors of hope and pure delight.
With each horizon, a new embrace,
In the horizon's arms, we find our place.

Mountains high and valleys low,
Our journey flows, a dance, a show.
Through fields of gold and skies so wide,
In boundless horizons, we confide.

We chase the dawn as shadows fade,
In this adventure, our fears are laid.
Every step whispers a silent song,
Together, in harmony, we belong.

As stars emerge in twilight's glow,
In the vast expanse, our spirits grow.
The universe sings, a timeless fuss,
Embracing the boundless horizons of us.

Fragments of Forever

In shattered light, we find our way,
Each memory a fragile ray.
In fragments scattered, love does bind,
A tapestry of heart and mind.

Every whisper, a piece reclaimed,
In moments passed, our hearts still named.
The laughter echoes, sweet and true,
In fragments of forever, me and you.

Underneath the starlit skies,
A dance of shadows, love never lies.
Each glance we share, a fleeting spark,
Illuminating pathways in the dark.

With every heartbeat, stories weave,
In threads of time, we dare believe.
Together we create, together mend,
In fragments of forever, never end.

In quiet corners of the soul,
Our pieces fit to make us whole.
Through every loss and every win,
In these fragments, forever begins.

Notes in a Melodic Journey

In tunes that drift on gentle air,
We find the rhythm, a song to share.
With every note that falls from grace,
A journey unfolds in time and space.

Underneath the starlit chorus,
A symphony that guides and floors us.
Through peaks and valleys, wild and free,
In this melody, you and me.

Each strum of strings, a heartbeat's plea,
In harmony, we learn to be.
Notes collide, then blend as one,
In the melodic journey, we have won.

With lyrics soft and dreams that fly,
We write our verses beneath the sky.
In every laugh and every tear,
The music swells when you are near.

A dance in time, a graceful sway,
In every moment, we dare to play.
Through life's song, we weave and twine,
Notes that linger, yours and mine.

The Bridge of Us

In shadows cast by twilight's glow,
We built a bridge, just you and me.
With whispered dreams that start to flow,
Our hearts entwined, we felt so free.

Through storms and trials, side by side,
We crossed each beam with faith and grace.
In every step, our trust implied,
A journey shared, a warm embrace.

The river wide, its waters deep,
Yet hand in hand, we face the tide.
The promises that we must keep,
In every tear, love still supplied.

As daylight fades, the stars will shine,
Our bridge remains, steadfast and true.
Through every challenge, you are mine,
Forever here, just us two.

Conversations in the Cosmos

Beneath the stars, our voices soar,
In cosmic whispers, dreams ignite.
Each moment shared, we seek for more,
In endless night, we find our light.

Galaxies spun in vibrant hues,
Our laughter dances through the air.
With every word, we chase the blues,
In constellations, love laid bare.

With twinkling eyes, we ponder fate,
The universe, a wondrous place.
In silent thoughts, we hesitate,
Yet find each other's warm embrace.

The planets course, a timeless track,
While comets streak, our dreams take flight.
In cosmic dance, we won't look back,
For in this space, our hearts unite.

Veils of Intimacy

In quiet corners, shadows blend,
We share our secrets, soft and low.
An unspoken bond begins to mend,
In veils of intimacy, we grow.

Each gentle touch, a fleeting spark,
Unraveling layers, skin on skin.
Through whispered words, we leave a mark,
In tender moments, love starts to spin.

With every sigh, our hearts collide,
In the sacred space, we lay bare.
The world outside fades, and inside,
We find the truth we long to share.

As night descends, we linger close,
Wrapped in warmth, our fears subside.
The deeper we dive, the more we chose,
In veils of love, where dreams abide.

Realms of Togetherness

In realms where trust and laughter meet,
We forge a path, hand in hand.
With each new day, our love's concrete,
Together in this promised land.

The sun will rise, and shadows fall,
Yet through it all, we find our way.
In every echo, through it all,
Our hearts will guide, come what may.

Through gardens lush, where flower blooms,
We wander deep, side by side.
In every scent, love softly looms,
In realms of joy, our hearts abide.

In quiet nights, our dreams align,
As stars above begin to gleam.
In every heartbeat, thoughts divine,
Together we create our dream.

Mosaic of Together

In colors bright and bold, we stand,
Creating art with heart and hand.
Each piece a story, time entwined,
In this mosaic, love defined.

Fragments shine in flawless glow,
Together crafted, love will grow.
With every touch and gentle care,
A masterpiece beyond compare.

We weave our lives in vibrant hues,
With every choice, we paint our views.
In laughter shared and tears we mend,
A tapestry that will not end.

Through shadows deep and light that breaks,
In unity, our spirit wakes.
Every moment, every chance,
A dance of souls in sweet romance.

So let us build this world anew,
In shapes and shades, in every hue.
Together, we will make it right,
A mosaic glowing in the light.

A Journey of Hands Held

Together we embark, you and I,
With hands held tight, we touch the sky.
Through every storm, through sunlit days,
We'll find our path, in countless ways.

With fingers laced, we face the climb,
Our hearts in sync, we keep the time.
Each step we take, a bond so strong,
In this grand waltz, we both belong.

From mountain peaks to valleys low,
With whispered dreams, we let love grow.
The road is ours, our souls aligned,
In every heartbeat, hope defined.

Through laughter shared and tears we shed,
With every word that's left unsaid.
Our journey flows like rivers wide,
With hands held tight, we'll turn the tide.

So let's embrace this chance we hold,
In stories written, yet untold.
Together we'll dance, through every bend,
A journey blessed, where hearts transcend.

Seasons of Our Love

Spring brings hope with blooms so bright,
In tender whispers, hearts take flight.
The world awakes from winter's hold,
In every petal, love unfolds.

Summer's warmth ignites our souls,
With laughter ringing, life extols.
Beneath the sun, we freely roam,
In every moment, we are home.

Autumn paints with strokes of gold,
In falling leaves, our stories told.
The crisp air wraps us, hand in hand,
In this soft glow, together stand.

Winter's chill may bring the night,
But in our hearts, there burns a light.
Through frosty breath and starry skies,
In love's embrace, the warmth does rise.

Each season dances, day by day,
In every shift, in every sway.
Together, we will weather all,
In seasons of love, we hear the call.

Beyond the Boundaries of Us

In the silence where whispers dwell,
A love extends, a secret spell.
Beyond the lines that time has drawn,
Our hearts unite, a new day dawns.

We break the walls, we chase the dreams,
In endless skies, we flow like streams.
Together soaring, higher, free,
In every heartbeat, you and me.

Beyond the stars, where shadows fade,
In fiery colors, love parades.
With every step, we forge our fate,
In unity, we resonate.

Through every trial, every test,
In love's embrace, we find our rest.
No limits bind our souls that thrive,
In this vast world, we will arrive.

So take my hand, let's span the space,
In every journey, feel our grace.
Beyond the boundaries, we will rise,
As one soul underneath the skies.

Melodies of Our Union

In the hush of twilight skies,
Love whispers soft and low.
Hearts entwined in sweet surprise,
Together we ebb and flow.

Every note's a tender kiss,
Harmony in every glance.
Life composed in perfect bliss,
In this rhythmic, stormy dance.

With each chord, our spirits soar,
Melodies that time won't break.
In the silence we explore,
Dreams shared for our future's sake.

Fingers laced on the guitar,
Strumming secrets of the night.
In our world, we travel far,
Echoes of love shining bright.

So let the music play on,
In every beat, we are one.
Through the dusk and into dawn,
Our union shines like the sun.

Niagara of Emotions

Tumbling down, the waters churn,
Passion cascades with pure grace.
Each drop tells a story learned,
In the rush, I see your face.

Golden hues in sunset's glow,
Raging tides, our feelings swell.
In this flow, we both will grow,
Waves of time, a vibrant spell.

Like a river, love does bend,
Carving paths through stone and heart.
Trust and hope, our sacred blend,
In the current, we won't part.

From the heights, the view astounds,
Nature sings our bold duet.
In the depths, our love resounds,
Never fading, never set.

As the seasons paint the land,
Our emotions bravely roar.
In this flow, we make a stand,
A Niagara forever more.

Riding the Waves of Us

On the ocean, we will glide,
Surfing dreams both near and far.
With you always by my side,
Every swell, our guiding star.

Tides may shift, but hearts remain,
Beneath the sun, we come alive.
Riding high on joy and pain,
In adventure, we will thrive.

Salty breezes kiss our skin,
Casting worries to the shore.
In this dance, we find our kin,
With each wave, we love much more.

Echoing the sea's embrace,
Catching whispers of the breeze.
In your eyes, I find my place,
Together, we ride with ease.

As we sail through life so wide,
Every motion harmonizes.
In this ocean, love is our guide,
Riding waves, our hearts arise.

Shadows of Together

In the twilight, shadows blend,
Echoes of a love once bold.
In the silence, hearts will mend,
Stories waiting to be told.

Hand in hand through dusk we walk,
Whispers cast in softest light.
Words unspoken, still we talk,
In the dark, our souls take flight.

Every step, a gentle pause,
Tracing memories we hold dear.
In the shadows, love gives cause,
Bringing forth our hopes, our fear.

Like the moonshine, soft and bright,
Guiding paths through veils of gray.
In the arms of starry night,
Together, we find our way.

With each dusk, a promise made,
In the shadows, light will grow.
Through the storm, love won't degrade,
In each other, we will glow.

Love's Multidimensional Canvas

Colors blend in our embrace,
Each hue a whisper of the soul.
Shades of laughter, strokes of grace,
On this canvas, we feel whole.

Textures weaving day and night,
Every thread a memory spun.
In the darkness, sparks of light,
Together, forever, as one.

Shapes of dreams come into view,
Every corner holds a tale.
Intertwined, just me and you,
Love's rich palette will not pale.

Vibrant moods, the heart's design,
Flickering like autumn leaves.
In this masterpiece, we're divine,
Each moment cherished, love believes.

Painted skies above us glow,
As we dance with time's soft tide.
In every heartbeat, love will flow,
On this canvas, we're allied.

Harmonious Hearts in Motion

Two hearts beat in rhythmic grace,
A melody that whispers near.
In the cadence, we find our place,
Every note a bond so dear.

Steps that twirl in perfect sync,
Weaving dreams on floors of light.
With each glance, we start to link,
In our dance, the world feels right.

The music swells, we lose our cares,
Moments echo all around.
In the hush, a love that dares,
Harmony in every sound.

Twinkling stars, a brilliant show,
Underneath a velvet sky.
Together, we let our spirits flow,
In this rhythm, we fly high.

Through the years, we'll sway and turn,
In this symphony of fate.
With each heartbeat, love will burn,
In our dance, we celebrate.

The Unfolding Narrative

Pages turn beneath our hands,
Every word a tale begun.
In this book, our love expands,
Story woven, two become one.

Chapters rich with joy and strife,
Plot twists that we face as one.
In the lines, we find our life,
Ink of dreams, our hearts are spun.

Characters crafted in the light,
Voices whisper through the night.
Together, we embrace the fight,
In this narrative, all feels right.

Memories penned with tender care,
Moments cherished, forever shared.
Every photo, love laid bare,
In this saga, we are dared.

Endings bloom to new beginnings,
A sequel waiting just ahead.
With each dawn, fresh love still singing,
In our story, hearts are led.

Together Beyond Time

In the shadows, time stands still,
Moments linger, soft and bright.
Eternity, a shared will,
In your arms, the world feels right.

Days may pass, years may flee,
Yet our bond will ever stay.
In this timeless harmony,
Love transcends both night and day.

Through the ages, hand in hand,
Every heartbeat speaks our truth.
In this dance, we understand,
Love's pure essence, eternal youth.

As the seasons softly change,
We embrace what comes our way.
In the whispers, nothing strange,
Together still, come what may.

Beyond the reach of mortal time,
Our souls entwined, forever bold.
In each laugh, in every rhyme,
A love story to unfold.

Boundless Horizons

In the morn, the sun will rise,
Painting skies with golden hues.
Mountains stand with silent pride,
Whispers of the wind ensues.

Oceans stretch, a vast embrace,
Waves that dance upon the shore.
Dreams take flight in open space,
Where the heart seeks evermore.

Stars above in endless flight,
Guiding souls through darkest night.
Journeys forge with every breath,
Life's embrace, a tale of depth.

Fields of green beneath our feet,
Paths that wander, hearts in sync.
Every moment feels complete,
In this world, no need to think.

Boundless love, it knows no end,
Horizons call to those who dare.
Together we shall always blend,
In the light, we find our prayer.

Tapestry of Together

Threads of laughter, woven tight,
Colors blend in perfect hue.
Each shared glance ignites the night,
In each moment, I find you.

Seasons change, yet here we stay,
Hand in hand, through thick and thin.
Every word a sweet ballet,
In this dance, we always win.

Memories stitched in golden seams,
Every heartbeat tells our tale.
In our dreams, we build our themes,
Love's sweet echo will not pale.

Through the storms, we find our way,
Guiding lights, our souls align.
In this life, come what may,
Together, we are truly fine.

Tapestry of hearts aglow,
In each stitch, the love we share.
Ever stronger, we will grow,
Bound by threads beyond compare.

Eternal Waves of Affection

On the shore, the waves will kiss,
Gentle tides that ebb and flow.
In each splash, a moment's bliss,
Boundless love, a constant glow.

Beneath the stars, the ocean sighs,
Whispers soft as breezes play.
In the night, our spirits rise,
Eternal waves that guide the way.

Footprints left upon the sand,
Tides may wash them, but we stay.
Hand in hand, we understand,
In our hearts, love's sweet ballet.

Every crash, a lullaby,
Nature's song in endless swell.
Through the years, as time slips by,
In this dance, we know so well.

Eternal waves, we find our peace,
As the sun dips low and sighs.
In this love, our joys increase,
Together, under endless skies.

Unbroken Paths of Us

In the dawn, we journey forth,
Steps on roads both paved and wild.
Every twist reveals our worth,
In this bond, we're nature's child.

Through the woods, the light will glint,
Leaves that dance with whispered grace.
In each moment, love's imprint,
Guiding us through time and space.

Mountains high, we face our fears,
Climbing ever toward the sun.
With each heartbeat, calm our tears,
In this life, we're never done.

At the crossroads, hands entwined,
Choices made, we forge our fate.
In our hearts, a love defined,
Paths unbroken, never late.

Unbroken paths lead us anew,
Every step, a song we sing.
Together, there's nothing we can't do,
In this life, our souls take wing.

In Each Other's Orbit

In silent space, we drift and soar,
Two souls entwined, forevermore.
A dance of light in the vast expanse,
Gravity pulls us into a trance.

Around and around, we twirl and glide,
In the constellations, love can't hide.
Every star whispers our sweet refrain,
Together we shine through joy and pain.

Through meteor showers, our hopes ignite,
In this embrace, we find our light.
The universe stretches, wide and bright,
In each other's orbit, we take flight.

Our hearts beat soft, a cosmic song,
In galaxies far, we still belong.
With every pulse, the world fades away,
In this eternal dance, we choose to stay.

Endless horizons call us near,
In the silence, our love is clear.
Boundless, the journey, forever to roam,
In each other's orbit, we find our home.

Stories Etched in the Stars

Each flicker tells a tale so old,
Of love's journey, brave and bold.
In twilight's breath, our dreams arise,
Stories etched in the vast skies.

Galaxies hum of battles fought,
Moments cherished, lessons taught.
Through every sorrow, laughter too,
The stars remember, just like you.

Wishes whispered on shooting stars,
Transported hearts, no matter how far.
We navigate the skies unknown,
Together, we're never alone.

Constellations map out our fate,
In the dark, we illuminate.
As time unfolds our sacred prose,
Stories written, in love, we compose.

In space, we find the tales we own,
In every heartbeat, love has grown.
Through the ages, we drift and sway,
Stories etched in stars light our way.

Tracing Love's Path

Through winding roads, our hearts take flight,
Every turn leads to pure delight.
With gentle hands, we trace the lines,
Mapping love in endless signs.

In every step, our shadows blend,
With whispered words, our souls ascend.
Through valleys deep and mountains high,
We walk together, you and I.

Each moment cherished, a step we take,
In love's embrace, we tend what breaks.
Through sunlit days and starry nights,
Tracing paths where true love ignites.

In every heartbeat, we find our way,
Moments crafted, come what may.
With every journey, our spirits soar,
Tracing love, forevermore.

Connected footsteps, we stride along,
In harmony, we sing our song.
With every mile, our bond grows strong,
Tracing love's path, where we belong.

Paths of Unison

Two roads converge beneath the moon,
In quiet whispers, hearts attune.
With gentle steps, we merge as one,
On paths of unison, love begun.

Through tangled woods and flowing streams,
We walk together, share our dreams.
With every glance, our spirits lift,
On this journey, love is the gift.

In the soft glow of dawn's first light,
Step by step, everything feels right.
With every heartbeat, we draw near,
On paths of unison, emotions clear.

In laughter shared and tears embraced,
We find the magic in every place.
Side by side, we brave the unknown,
Together, we've beautifully grown.

As stars align and seasons change,
Our hearts entwined, never estranged.
In every moment, our love will shine,
On paths of unison, forever entwined.

Eternal Threads Weaving Time

In the tapestry of night, we weave,
Threads of silver and gold, they believe.
Every moment a stitch, every breath a rhyme,
Binding our souls through the fabric of time.

Across the loom where shadows play,
Patterns emerge with light's soft sway.
With each heartbeat, a design refined,
Eternal threads in our hearts entwined.

Moments fade but memories stay,
Woven together, come what may.
In the silence, a whisper flows,
Time's gentle hand, as the river goes.

Through the ages, we dance in light,
Guided by stars in the quiet night.
With every dawn, our tales unfurl,
In the fabric of life, we find our world.

Forever stitched in creation's weave,
In every pattern, our hearts believe.
As long as the stars in the sky align,
We'll cherish the threads that intertwine.

Whispers Through Cycles

In the hush of dawn, whispers begin,
Echoes of dreams carried on the wind.
Through cycles of seasons, we learn to trust,
Nature's soft voice speaks in starlit dust.

Colors of autumn paint our skies,
While winter's silence wraps the cries.
Each heartbeat matches the fluttering leaves,
Life's rhythms teach what the spirit believes.

With spring, the blooms rise in grace,
Renewed hope finds its cherished place.
In summer's warmth, laughter spills free,
Whispers of love in the rustling tree.

In silence we gather, in cycles we grow,
Through every heartbeat, the stories flow.
Moments compiled in the sands of time,
Whispers within, a gentle chime.

So let us embrace the ebb and flow,
In whispers of cycles, our spirits glow.
Together we dance, as seasons align,
In the symphony of life, our souls entwine.

Cadence of Our Days

In morning light, we rise anew,
With dreams afresh, the day in view.
The clock ticks on, a rhythmic song,
In every heart, where we belong.

Moments pass like whispers soft,
In laughter's embrace, we drift aloft.
Time weaves tales in colors bright,
Guiding us through day and night.

With every laugh, a memory blooms,
In quiet corners, love consumes.
We dance to beats we've yet to know,
As life unfolds in gentle flow.

Through trials faced, we find our way,
In shadows long, we learn to play.
The cadence strong, it holds us near,
In every heartbeat, you are here.

So let us cherish every beat,
In whispered truths and moments sweet.
For in the rhythm, we are found,
As life's own melody surrounds.

Roots and Wings

In soil deep, our roots entwine,
Holding fast to love divine.
From humble earth, we reach for skies,
In every dream, our spirit flies.

With wings unfurled, we chase the sun,
In every heart, there lies the run.
The balance held, a sacred trust,
To rise and soar, to hope, we must.

Through storms we weather, storms we face,
In unity, we find our place.
Both anchored strong and free to roam,
In bond of love, we find our home.

The tree of life, it stands so tall,
Through seasons change, we hear the call.
With roots so deep, and wings so wide,
In harmony, we turn the tide.

So take my hand, let's journey far,
With roots and wings, we'll chase the stars.
In every sunset, every dawn,
Together still, we keep pressing on.

Timeless Conversations

In whispered tones beneath the stars,
We share our dreams, our hopes, our scars.
With every word, a bridge we build,
In silent pauses, hearts fulfilled.

The clock may tick, yet time stands still,
In conversations sweet, we find our thrill.
Stories woven with threads of grace,
In every glance, our sacred space.

From dawn till dusk, our voices blend,
In laughter shared, our souls extend.
In every sigh, a world unfolds,
In every touch, our love retold.

Through distances vast, we stay entwined,
In memories cherished, we never mind.
For in the words that dance and play,
We shape the night, we greet the day.

Together still, our whispers last,
In timeless talks, we've forged the past.
In threads unseen, we're never part,
For in this bond, we share one heart.

Beyond the Surface of Time

In every heartbeat, echoes flow,
In moments past, we still can grow.
Beyond the ticks of fleeting hours,
Lie stories rich, like blooming flowers.

We sail through days, both calm and wild,
In every smile, a memory filed.
Beyond the veil of what we see,
Lies hidden depth, a melody.

With every dawn, new visions rise,
In shadows cast, we find the prize.
Time bends gently, like a soft sigh,
Inviting all to dream and fly.

Through layers thick, the truth unfolds,
In tales untold, our fate beholds.
So take my hand, let's journey far,
Beyond the surface, just like stars.

In cosmic dance, we find our place,
In timeless space, we embrace grace.
With every moment, we intertwine,
Beyond the surface, forever shine.

Symmetry in Our Hearts

In quiet whispers, we align,
Two hearts in rhythm, so divine.
With every beat, a secret song,
A mirrored dance where we belong.

Eyes meet softly, spark ignites,
Two souls entwined on starry nights.
A perfect balance, give and take,
In every promise, love awake.

Moments shared, a timeless thread,
With every glance, words left unsaid.
Together we weave, worlds combine,
In our embrace, the stars align.

Through laughter's echo, pain's refrain,
Mutual shelter from the rain.
With gentle grace, we forge our way,
A symphony in love's ballet.

Forever twirling, side by side,
In this grand dance, our souls abide.
A tapestry of dreams we spin,
In symmetry, where love begins.

Dance of Two Souls

Under moonlight, we take the floor,
With every step, we long for more.
Two souls collide in silken grace,
Each movement tells our heart's embrace.

The world dissolves, it's just us two,
In perfect rhythm, dreams come true.
With every twirl, we lose the night,
Boundless joy in shared delight.

In gentle whispers, we confess,
Love unfolds in its soft caress.
A dance that speaks, without a word,
In silent vows, our hearts concurred.

The tempo quickens, pulses race,
Two bodies move, a sacred space.
In every turn, we intertwine,
A fusion rare, so pure, divine.

As dawn approaches, shadows wane,
In our embrace, we'll meet again.
For in this dance, our spirits soar,
Eternally, we'll seek for more.

Moments Like Starlight

In fleeting breaths, we find our bliss,
Each moment sparkles, a stolen kiss.
Like starlight pierces through the gray,
You make the ordinary sway.

With laughter's echo, time stands still,
In simple joys, our hearts fulfill.
The world expands in shadows cast,
Each memory shines, a spell is cast.

Through golden mornings, dusk's embrace,
We chase the light at our own pace.
In every heartbeat, love ignites,
Moments linger in endless nights.

Together we write our story bright,
With every glance, we conquer fright.
In starlit hours, dreams take flight,
Unraveling magic, pure and light.

These moments weave a tapestry,
From thread of you and thread of me.
In stardust glow, we make our mark,
In this vast universe, we spark.

Time's Embrace

The clock ticks softly, a gentle chime,
In every second, we find our rhyme.
Moments fleeting, like grains of sand,
Yet in your arms, I understand.

We chase the hours, yet leave them still,
In shared laughter, we bend our will.
Time softly bends in love's sweet thrall,
With you, I'm free, I have it all.

As seasons turn and shadows fall,
With you beside me, I fear no call.
Together we dance through joy and strife,
In every heartbeat, a pulse of life.

Time's embrace cradles us, so dear,
Each precious moment, we'll hold near.
In whispers shared and daybreak's light,
Two souls entwined, forever right.

For in your gaze, eternity gleams,
A timeline woven through our dreams.
As moments gather, we'll stand as one,
In time's embrace, we shine like sun.

Synchronized Heartbeats

In shadows where whispers dwell,
Two souls dance in a silent spell.
Heartbeat echoes soft and low,
A rhythm only they can know.

In every glance a promise lies,
Unraveling dreams beneath the skies.
With every touch, the world fades out,
Love's melody, their only shout.

In twilight's glow, they stand as one,
A canvas painted with the sun.
Time ceases in their warm embrace,
A sacred moment, a cherished space.

Two heartbeats beating as a song,
In harmony, where they belong.
With each moment, they intertwine,
An endless dance, a love divine.

Love's Grand Continuum

Across the ages, like a stream,
Love flows gently, a timeless dream.
Through valleys deep and hills so high,
An endless journey under the sky.

In moments shared, the world aligns,
Each heartbeat crafting perfect lines.
With laughter bright, they light the night,
Turning whispers into pure delight.

Through seasons change, love does not fade,
In every memory, paths are laid.
Wrapped in warmth, they find their way,
In love's embrace, forever stay.

With every dawn, a new refrain,
In every storm, a gentle rain.
Together, they weave their story grand,
In love's continuum, hand in hand.

Celestial Bonds of Affection

Under starlight, they find their place,
In the cosmos, a sweet embrace.
Constellations gleam with delight,
Whispering secrets into the night.

Their hearts align like planets in tune,
Creating harmony beneath the moon.
In every sigh, the universe sways,
Dancing to love's eternal plays.

Galaxies swirl, and time holds still,
As stardust dreams their wishes fulfill.
In the quiet depths of endless space,
They forge their bond, a sacred grace.

Two souls intertwined in cosmic dance,
In the fabric of fate, they take a chance.
With every heartbeat, they ignite the night,
In celestial bonds, their love takes flight.

Perpetual Embrace

In an ocean of moments where time stands still,
Two hearts entwined, a sacred will.
With open arms, they share the light,
In perpetual embrace, their souls take flight.

With every whisper, the world retreats,
In love's warm glow, each heartbeat meets.
Crafting memories in softest hues,
A timeless tapestry, love's muse.

Hand in hand, they face the dawn,
In quiet strength, a bond is drawn.
Through laughter and tears, they journey on,
In every shadow, love responds.

In the stillness of night, their dreams align,
In the warmth of each other, forever shine.
A story written in starlit grace,
In life's embrace, they find their place.

The Flow of We

In moments shared, we drift as one,
Like rivers merging, under the sun.
Together we dance, in harmony sweet,
Our hearts entwined, where love's currents meet.

Through storms and calm, hand in hand we go,
Facing the tides, together we flow.
With every wave, our laughter ignites,
In the ebb and flow, our spirits take flight.

In whispers gentle, our stories unfold,
In the flow of we, true love is told.
As seasons change, our bond remains strong,
In the river of life, where we both belong.

Through the wilderness, paths intertwined,
In the magic of us, true love we find.
With each gentle ripple, our dreams take form,
In the flow of we, where hearts are warm.

So let the waters guide us afar,
With love as our compass, our guiding star.
In the flow of we, forever we'll roam,
In the heart of each other, we find our home.

Tides of Time Unfolding

In the sands of time, we leave our mark,
With every wave, igniting the spark.
As tides roll in, our hearts rewind,
In the rhythm of life, our souls aligned.

Moments fade like whispers in the breeze,
Yet in their essence, we find our ease.
Like tides of time, they rise and fall,
Yet through it all, together we stand tall.

With every dawn, new stories to tell,
In the ocean of dreams, we cast our spell.
Through twilight's grace, the colors ignite,
In the canvas of time, we find our light.

The moonlight whispers, guiding our way,
Through shifting sands, we choose to stay.
In the dance of the tides, we brave the unknown,
With every heartbeat, our love has grown.

As we sail through the currents of fate,
In the tides of time, we celebrate.
With each passing wave, a new chance to find,
In the voyage of life, your hand in mine.

Boundless Adventures Together

In every sunrise, a journey begins,
With laughter and joy, through thick and thin.
Hand in hand, we seek the unknown,
In boundless adventures, our love has grown.

Across mountain peaks, we chase the skies,
With hearts full of hope, our spirits rise.
Through valleys deep, we find our way,
In the magic of moments, come what may.

With every step, a new story unfolds,
In the treasure of memories, our hearts hold.
From the whispers of forests to oceans wide,
In boundless adventures, we take pride.

As stars light the night, we dream and explore,
With courage and love, we long for more.
In the dance of the wild, we find our voice,
In the rhythm of life, we rejoice.

Together we wander, forever as one,
In the embrace of the world, our hearts run.
Through every adventure, my dear, you'll see,
In this journey of us, we're forever free.

Whispers Across Infinity

Through the silence of space, our voices collide,
In whispers of love, where dreams cannot hide.
Across the vast cosmos, our feelings ignite,
In the depths of the stars, we find our light.

Every heartbeat echoes, a timeless refrain,
In the dance of existence, through joy and pain.
In galaxies spinning, our souls intertwine,
In whispers across infinity, you are mine.

The cosmos embraces, our spirits take flight,
With each gentle breeze, we soar to new heights.
In the tapestry woven, our colors blend,
In whispers of love that never will end.

Through the fabric of time, we journey hand in hand,
In the symphony of stars, we make our stand.
With every breath, a promise to keep,
In whispers across infinity, our love runs deep.

So as we traverse through the galaxies wide,
In the heart of the universe, we will reside.
In the silence of space, forever we'll be,
In whispers of love, just you and me.

Tides of Intimacy

In the moon's soft glow, we sway,
Captured in the night's embrace,
Waves of whispers, hearts at play,
Calm and wild in this sacred space.

Gentle touch, our fingers dance,
Threads of warmth, they intertwine,
Each heartbeat sings a sweet romance,
Lost in moments, yours and mine.

The ocean pulls, we drift as one,
Secrets shared beneath the stars,
In this tide, our fears are gone,
Boundless love, no more scars.

Time stands still, a breath, a sigh,
In your gaze, the world fades out,
Together, beneath the sky,
Feeling safe, erasing doubt.

As dawn breaks, we greet the light,
Memories painted on the shore,
In each wave, our spirits flight,
Forever yours, forevermore.

Mosaic of Affection

Each piece a story, a hue, a voice,
Laid together, a vibrant whole,
In this collage, there is choice,
A tapestry spun from the soul.

Fragments of laughter, smiles like sun,
Moments captured, gleaming bright,
In every shard, heartbeats run,
Crafting love from dark and light.

With gentle hands, we fit and mold,
Colors blending, no gap to see,
A masterpiece in our hold,
United in this harmony.

Through storms and quiet, we remain,
A beauty born from every test,
Together weathering joy and pain,
In this mosaic, we are blessed.

With love's embrace, we take our flight,
A dance of dreams, a shining path,
In every piece, we find our light,
Bound by love's unyielding math.

Bound by Stars

Beneath the cosmos, we align,
Galaxies whisper in the night,
In the vastness, your heart is mine,
Fate has drawn our paths in light.

Constellations weave our fate,
A dance of souls through cosmic dust,
In this moment, we create,
A universe built on trust.

Orbiting dreams, our minds take flight,
In every heartbeat, a spark resides,
With you, my love, the world feels right,
Together, through the starlit tides.

Eclipsed in shadows, we'll still shine,
Illuminated by love's embrace,
Every twinkle is a sign,
That we've found our sacred place.

As comets trail and planets play,
In this dance, we lose all fear,
Hand in hand, we chart our way,
In the starlight, you are near.

Reflections of Togetherness

In the glassy lake, we see,
Two souls dancing in the flow,
Reflections merge, you and me,
Together, where the waters glow.

With every ripple, laughter streams,
Echos of joy, a sweet refrain,
In dreams we build, our hearts' themes,
Creating magic from the mundane.

Through seasons changing, we hold tight,
Hand in hand, we weather storms,
In every shadow, find the light,
Our love, the warmth that transforms.

In mirrored depths, our stories blend,
Moments captured, love's embrace,
Every glance, a precious send,
In this journey, time's sweet grace.

With each dawning day anew,
We find our strength, a bond secured,
In reflections, vivid and true,
Together, our hearts reassured.

Unfurling Love's Scroll

In whispers soft, the scroll unfurls,
A tale of hearts, in tender swirls.
Each line a promise, each word a song,
In love's embrace, where we belong.

With sunlight's touch and moonlight's grace,
We weave our dreams, we find our place.
Through every chapter, hand in hand,
Together we rise, together we stand.

The ink of time stains every page,
Each moment lived, we set the stage.
With laughter, tears, and silent vows,
Our love a tapestry, woven now.

As seasons turn and years do blend,
Through every trial, our hearts amend.
In quiet nights, in mornings bright,
Our love's scroll dances in the light.

And when the final verse is penned,
We'll cherish each moment, never end.
In the story of us, forever we'll dwell,
In love's sweet embrace, unfurling well.

Navigating Infinity

Stars align in quiet skies,
Mapping dreams where silence lies.
We sail the seas of endless night,
Guided by love's constant light.

With every heartbeat, time expands,
In the vastness, two souls stand.
Threads of fate begin to weave,
In this dance, we shall believe.

Across the void, through endless space,
Together we chase, we dare, we grace.
A journey long, yet time stands still,
In the depths of hearts, we feel the thrill.

Galaxies swirl, and comets blaze,
In our love, we find our ways.
Through cosmic storms, our voices soar,
In the infinite, we seek more.

In whispers soft, we find our home,
Navigating where love can roam.
In every moment, a new sunrise,
In infinity's arms, we shall rise.

Frequency of Heartbeats

In the silence, our hearts collide,
A rhythm steady, love as our guide.
With every pulse, a story told,
In the frequency, our lives unfold.

Echoes of laughter, whispers of dreams,
Together we flow like gentle streams.
A symphony played on life's great stage,
In the dance of hearts, we engage.

Through highs and lows, our song persists,
In the hum of life, we coexist.
With every beat, a bond so deep,
In the frequency, our secrets keep.

Frequencies blend, they rise, they fall,
In love's embrace, we hear the call.
In every moment, a brand new start,
In this rhythm, we share our heart.

As time flows on, we'll keep the tune,
Beneath the stars, beneath the moon.
In the cadence of life, we'll meet life's art,
Forever entwined, in heartbeat's heart.

Paired in Perpetuity

In the dance of time, we find our way,
Paired in perpetuity, come what may.
With every glance, a spark ignites,
In the shared silence, our love ignites.

Through storms and sun, we journey on,
In every dusk, we greet the dawn.
With hands so warm, we brave the cold,
In the stories shared, our love is told.

In quiet moments, in laughter's cheer,
We find our strength, there's nothing to fear.
As seasons change, our roots run deep,
In this bond, our dreams we keep.

With whispered words, in the night's embrace,
We carve our path, we find our place.
Paired like stars in the vast above,
In this union, we feel the love.

As years drift by, we'll hold so tight,
In every heartbeat, our souls take flight.
Together forever, as time flows free,
In love's sweet dance, just you and me.

The Unfolding of Us

In twilight's glow, we start to mend,
Two wandering souls, a journey to blend.
With whispered dreams, we chase the light,
Together we stand, hearts burning bright.

Through valleys deep, we face the storm,
Hand in hand, our spirits warm.
The tapestry of us, woven tight,
In every shadow, we find our flight.

Mountains rise, but we will climb,
With every breath, we share our time.
The whispers of love echo through years,
In laughter, in silence, through all our fears.

The stars align, our paths entwined,
In the chaos of life, solace we find.
Each moment a brush, painting our way,
In the masterpiece of love, we choose to stay.

With every heartbeat, a story unfolds,
In the book of us, a tale retold.
The unending journey, a passion so true,
Forever and ever, just me and you.

An Odyssey of Heartbeats

In the silence, we hear the call,
Of every heartbeat, together we fall.
Like waves caress the shore with grace,
Our love, a timeless waltz in space.

Across the night, the moon shines bright,
Guiding our hearts in the softest light.
Through shadows long, we chase the dawn,
In every sigh, a new hope drawn.

With courage, we leap into the unknown,
In the garden of dreams, our seeds are sown.
Every pulse a promise, every gaze a spark,
In the odyssey of us, we light the dark.

Through storms we sail, in calm we rest,
With open hearts, we feel so blessed.
Each heartbeat echoes, a rhythm divine,
In the symphony of love, our spirits align.

Together we wander, no end in sight,
In the embrace of love, we find our flight.
With every adventure, our journey renews,
In the odyssey of heartbeats, it's me and you.

In the Heart's Embrace

In a gentle hush, love takes its form,
Nestled closely, away from the storm.
With hands entwined, we close our eyes,
Lost in the warmth, where true love lies.

The world fades out, just you and I,
In the heart's embrace, we learn to fly.
Moments we treasure, softly we share,
In every heartbeat, a whispered prayer.

Through every challenge, side by side,
In joy and sorrow, our love won't hide.
With each new dawn, we greet the day,
In the heart's embrace, we find our way.

Under the stars, dreams take flight,
In the quiet stillness of the night.
Together we weave the life we choose,
In the heart's embrace, we can't lose.

As seasons change, our love will grow,
In the garden of dreams, we share and sow.
With every heartbeat, forever stays,
In the heart's embrace, love gently sways.

Endless Echoes of Us

In the depths of night, whispers unfold,
Echoes of love in stories retold.
With every heartbeat, a rhythm we find,
In the endless dance of two hearts aligned.

Through laughter and tears, we craft our tale,
In the winds of time, our love will sail.
From mountain tops to valleys below,
The echoes of us in the stillness grow.

In quiet moments, we share our dreams,
With open hearts, nothing's as it seems.
Like shadows at dusk, we fade and merge,
In the endless echoes, our spirits surge.

With every sunset, a promise made,
In the canvas of dusk, our fears will fade.
Through every storm, our bond will last,
In the endless echoes, hold on to the past.

Together we wander where few dare to go,
In the distance, our love's gentle glow.
With every heartbeat, forever must be,
In the endless echoes of you and me.

Embracing the Endless

In a realm where dreams entwine,
Stars whisper softly, a secret divine.
Each moment, a spark, brightly aglow,
Time dances lightly, in ebb and flow.

Hands reach out to the vast unknown,
With courage sown in hearts so grown.
Boundless skies, colors ablaze,
Life unfolds in myriad ways.

Waves of wonder, gently unfold,
Stories of heart in each thread told.
The journey stretches, love's radiant light,
Together we soar, through day and night.

Embrace the now, let go of the past,
In this moment, find joy that lasts.
Every heartbeat, every shared glance,
In this endless dance, we take our chance.

With every breath, a promise made,
In the heart's deep garden, dreams cascade.
Infinite whispers guide our way,
Embracing the endless, come what may.

Duality in Resonance

In shadows cast by the moon's soft light,
Day meets night in an elegant fight.
Two sides of a coin, both shining bright,
In duality's dance, we find our sight.

Harmony speaks in a silent tongue,
In every soul, the melody's sung.
Hope and despair, woven in voice,
In the tapestry of life, we rejoice.

Each heartbeat echoes a rhythmic plea,
In the depths of silence, we are free.
To understand love, one must know loss,
The beauty of life, in both gain and cross.

Fragile blooms in the garden of fate,
Resonating whispers, never too late.
In the pull of opposites, we find our way,
Guided by shadows, we move through the gray.

Creation thrives in the balance we seek,
In laughter and tears, our spirits speak.
Hand in hand with the light and the dark,
In this duality, we leave our mark.

Journey of Forever

Footsteps upon a winding road,
Carrying dreams where stories flowed.
With each turn, a new chapter unfolds,
The journey of forever in paths untold.

Mountains rise high, valleys below,
With every challenge, our courage will grow.
In the whispering winds, we hear the call,
A promise of purpose that bonds us all.

Stars above chart a course so bright,
Guiding our hearts through the depths of night.
With hope in our pockets and love in our hands,
We traverse the vast and uncharted lands.

Time may unfold like a delicate bloom,
Within its embrace, we find room.
Eternity sings in the rhythm of life,
A journey of forever, ignoring the strife.

When paths merge together, destinies blend,
In each other's warmth, we learn to ascend.
Bound by a vision, hearts beat as one,
On this journey of forever, we've only begun.

Intertwined Destinies

Life's gentle web weaves stories near,
In every thread, our souls appear.
Intertwined destinies, fates align,
In the dance of time, our spirits shine.

Through trials faced and laughter shared,
In the tapestry of hope, we dared.
Each bond we forge, a link so strong,
An anthem of unity, our shared song.

With every heartbeat, a tale unfolds,
In the silence of night, our truth beholds.
Voices whisper, calling us close,
In each other's arms, we find purpose most.

Stars above witness our dreams take flight,
With open hearts, we embrace the night.
In the garden of life, we plant our seeds,
Intertwined destinies, fulfilling our needs.

Together we wander through valleys and hills,
With laughter and love, the world fulfills.
Life's intricate web of joy and pain,
In the dance of destiny, love will remain.

Harmony in the Cosmos

Stars whisper secrets, bright and clear,
Galaxies dance, drawing us near.
In the silence, we find our place,
Unified in this vast, cosmic space.

Waves of stardust glimmer and flow,
Time's gentle hand guides us to know.
In the stillness, our hearts align,
Echoes of space become divine.

The universe sings in tones profound,
In its embrace, peace can be found.
Each heartbeat a note, rich and full,
A symphony played, both calm and dull.

From the nebulae to the black holes,
All of existence, intertwined souls.
Harmony whispers through the night,
Guiding us home, pure and bright.

As we gaze at the celestial tide,
In each star, our dreams abide.
Together, forever, we shall roam,
In cosmic love, we find our home.

The Unseen Bond

Through silent glances, hearts connect,
In the depths, we find respect.
Invisible threads bind us tight,
Holding us close, day and night.

Words unspoken, yet understood,
In shared moments, our spirits stood.
In laughter and in gentle tears,
Love lingers on, conquering fears.

The warmth between us softly glows,
In quiet times, our affection shows.
No need for words, just a gentle touch,
In this unseen bond, we feel so much.

In the chaos, we find our peace,
A timeless connection, that will not cease.
Through life's journeys, we walk as one,
With every step, our hearts have spun.

Cherished moments, forever sealed,
In this love, we are revealed.
Through the storms, through the calm,
Our unseen bond, a healing balm.

Spirals of Shared Dreams

In twilight's glow, our dreams unfold,
Whispers of futures yet untold.
With each spin, we rise and fall,
In spirals of hope, we answer the call.

Through tangled paths, together we weave,
In the fabric of life, we believe.
Visions dance, like shadows in flight,
Illuminated by the soft moonlight.

Hand in hand, we journey far,
Chasing echoes of a distant star.
Each step a promise, each breath a start,
In the tapestry of dreams, we play our part.

Every turn a story, a memory spun,
In the cycle of time, we are never done.
United in passion, we shall explore,
Finding new worlds, forevermore.

As night embraces the fading day,
In spirals of dreams, we find our way.
With every heartbeat, our hopes ignite,
Together we shine, as day turns to night.

Reflections in a Shared Journey

Mirrored paths, where our stories blend,
In shadows cast, we find a friend.
Each turn reveals a brand new face,
In this shared journey, our rightful place.

Through valleys low and mountains high,
We walk together, side by side.
In laughter and trials, our spirits grow,
Roots intertwined, steady and slow.

With every challenge, we learn to thrive,
In the dance of life, we feel alive.
Reflections of love in each other's eyes,
In moments of doubt, our faith never dies.

Beneath the stars, we chart our way,
Through the night leading into day.
With courage, we face the unknown path,
In unity found, we embrace our wrath.

Through time and space, our hearts collide,
In this journey, you are my guide.
Each footstep taken, a note in the song,
In the symphony of life, together we belong.

Love's Uncharted Voyage

In a sea of stars we drift,
Hearts sailing on tender dreams,
Charting courses through soft whispers,
Navigating by love's light beams.

Unfamiliar shores arise,
Waves crash with a gentle sigh,
Together we face the horizon,
In this journey, you and I.

Through storms that test our will,
We hold tight, never to part,
Anchoring in trust's deep harbor,
As the compass of our hearts.

Every sunset paints our sky,
Golden hues of our shared fate,
With every dawn, a new promise,
In love's embrace, we celebrate.

So let the winds of fate blow strong,
With courage, we sail this sea,
For in this voyage, we belong,
Two souls bound, forever free.

Garden of Shared Memories

In a garden where time stands still,
Blooming flowers whisper your name,
Petals dance in the softest breeze,
Each moment cherished, never the same.

Paths entwined, we wander slow,
Discovering secrets beneath the leaves,
Sunlight filters through the branches,
In this haven, our heart believes.

The sound of laughter fills the air,
Songs of joy, sweet melodies,
With every glance, a spark ignites,
In the fragrance of blooming peace.

Seasons change, yet love remains,
Roots growing deeper, intertwined,
Through every storm and gentle rain,
In this garden, our hearts aligned.

So let us nurture what we've sown,
As memories blossom, ever bright,
In this sacred space we've grown,
Together, we bask in the light.

Time's Embrace

Beneath the clock's relentless tick,
Moments linger, then swiftly fade,
Yet in your arms, I find my peace,
As time's embrace, our hearts have made.

Days blend into nights of gold,
Whispers tracing memories dear,
Each second held, a treasure told,
In the silence, I feel you near.

Though seasons shift and shadows play,
Our laughter echoes through the years,
In every tear, in every smile,
Love conquers all, surpasses fears.

As the sands of time slip by,
We gather moments, hand in hand,
In this dance, we'll never say goodbye,
Time's embrace, a love so grand.

Forever anchored in this space,
No distance can our bond erase,
In every heartbeat, life's sweet grace,
Together, we define our pace.

Entangled Horizons

When the sun meets the ocean's kiss,
Horizons stretch where dreams take flight,
In your eyes, I see the morning,
A canvas painted with pure light.

Each wave that crashes on the shore,
Calls our spirits to intertwine,
In this vast world, we explore,
Together, forever, you are mine.

The stars align in cosmic dance,
As pathways blend, our souls in tune,
In this twilight's gentle glance,
We find our place beneath the moon.

Through every dusk and dawn anew,
The future whispers soft and clear,
With open hearts, we'll chase what's true,
Entangled horizons, love sincere.

So let the voyage carry on,
With faith as our guiding star,
In every breath, a silent song,
Our love, the compass, near or far.

Embracing Change

Leaves fall gently to the ground,
A silent song of seasons round.
With each new breath, we let it go,
In change, a hidden beauty grows.

The river flows, it bends and sways,
Reflecting light in shifting rays.
Each moment brings a fresh new chance,
In life's grand dance, we learn to prance.

From shadows cast, new paths arise,
Awakening hopes beneath the skies.
Embrace the shift, let worries fade,
In transformation, dreams are made.

As seasons turn, we find our way,
In letting go, we learn to stay.
The heart remembers, the mind still learns,
In the ebb and flow, true wisdom burns.

With open arms, we face the dawn,
Each day's a gift, a brand new song.
In every change, a spark ignites,
Leading us to wondrous heights.

Holding Tight

In quiet moments, hands entwined,
We find our peace, two souls aligned.
A whispered word, a gentle sigh,
In this warm embrace, we fly high.

Through storms that rage and shadows loom,
Together we create our room.
A sanctuary built on trust,
In love's embrace, it's fair and just.

With every laugh, each shared delight,
We hold our dreams, our hearts ignite.
Through trials faced, we stand as one,
In unity, our battles won.

With every tear, we learn to grow,
In joy and sorrow, love will flow.
We write our story, day by day,
In the beauty of this dance, we sway.

As years unfold, our bond will thrive,
In every heartbeat, love's alive.
With trust and warmth, we face the night,
In each other's arms, we hold on tight.

Sweet Labyrinths of Connection

In the maze of laughter, we roam,
Every twist leads us back home.
Paths of kindness, threads of grace,
In each encounter, a warm embrace.

Stories told in glances shared,
In silence speaks how much we cared.
A tapestry woven, heartstrings entwined,
In sweet labyrinths, our hearts aligned.

Through every turn, new faces greet,
In the chaos, there's rhythm and beat.
Connections bloom, like flowers in spring,
In this dance of life, our spirits sing.

Hand in hand, we explore the dawn,
In every shadow, a light is drawn.
With open hearts, we welcome the chance,
In sweet connections, we find our dance.

Together we wander, hand in hand,
Through the gardens of dreams, across the land.
Each moment a treasure, each laugh a key,
In labyrinths sweet, we're forever free.

Through the Lens of Us

In every snapshot, memories hold,
A story of love in frames of gold.
Through the lens, we see our truth,
In every moment, we find our youth.

Captured smiles, the warmth of your gaze,
In gentle whispers, our hearts ablaze.
Through life's journey, both near and far,
Together we shine, our guiding star.

In reflection, we glimpse what's real,
Every heartbreak, every joyful reel.
Through the lens, we shape our fate,
With each captured moment, we celebrate.

In the blur of life, we stand so still,
Through laughter and tears, we find our will.
In every focus, there's a spark divine,
Through the lens of us, our hearts align.

As time unfolds, our stories blend,
In each frozen moment, love won't end.
Through the lens we hold, forever true,
In every picture, it's me and you.

A Timeless Tapestry

With threads of gold and shades so bright,
We weave our dreams in soft moonlight.
In every stitch, a tale unfolds,
Of love and laughter, of warmth and holds.

Each color speaks of moments shared,
In this tapestry, we've truly dared.
Woven tightly, we find our way,
In life's grand loom, we seize the day.

Through every tear and joyful thread,
A legacy of love is spread.
In this design, our hearts collide,
In every pattern, stories abide.

As seasons change, our threads adapt,
In every challenge, a bond is strapped.
Through time's embrace, we'll always find,
In this tapestry, our souls aligned.

With each new dawn, we add our hues,
A canvas created of all we choose.
Hand in hand, we craft our fate,
In a timeless tapestry, we celebrate.

Echoing Hearts in Space

In the silence of the stars,
Two hearts send their calls,
Echoes float through the dark,
Breaking down distant walls.

Galaxies whisper softly,
As dreams begin to soar,
A dance of cosmic lovers,
Yearning for evermore.

Constellations align,
Guiding them through the night,
Fate weaves their stories,
With threads of pure light.

Their voices meld like stardust,
Painting skies with their songs,
In the vastness of the cosmos,
Together they belong.

In the universe's cradle,
Love's gravity holds tight,
Two souls become a symphony,
In the endless void of night.

Canvas of Two Lives

With each brushstroke of fate,
A portrait starts to form,
Two lives entwined in color,
Creating a new norm.

Shades of laughter and sorrow,
Blend in vibrant hues,
A masterpiece revealing,
The stories we choose.

Every line tells a journey,
Each curve, a shared smile,
In the gallery of moments,
They linger for a while.

Time reveals the layers,
As they grow side by side,
A canvas rich with beauty,
In love, they confide.

Together they'll keep painting,
A vision ever bright,
In the art of their living,
Love is their guiding light.

Love Beyond the Veil

In whispers of the twilight,
Their spirits often meet,
Through shadows, they still wander,
In silence, hearts can speak.

They dance among the ethereal,
With touches light as air,
A bond that breaks all barriers,
In realms beyond compare.

Unseen yet deeply felt,
Their love defies the night,
Beyond the fragile veil,
Their souls embrace the light.

In dreams, they find each other,
Through echoes soft and clear,
Together in the stillness,
Their love will persevere.

As stars light up the heavens,
With every fleeting glance,
They weave a thread of comfort,
In a cosmic dance.

Threads of Time Interwoven

Two lives, a tapestry,
Woven through pleasure and pain,
Each thread a whispered moment,
In sunshine and in rain.

The fabric holds their laughter,
And every tear they've shed,
In the loom of shared memories,
Their journey brightly spread.

A stitching of desires,
In patterns bold and fine,
From the warp to the weft,
They craft a love divine.

Through seasons of their story,
They thread the needle true,
Creating a lasting bond,
In every shade and hue.

As time unfolds their story,
With every passing year,
Their woven hearts grow stronger,
In love, they persevere.

The Dance of Us in Infinity

In shadows we sway, lost in the night,
With whispers of stars, our hearts take flight.
The moonlight wraps us in a silken thread,
Together we twirl, where dreams are bred.

Your laughter a melody, soft and clear,
It echoes through time, drawing me near.
With every step, we let the world fade,
In this endless waltz, our fears are laid.

The universe spins, yet we stand still,
Bound by a rhythm that gives us thrill.
Each heartbeat syncs in a cosmic dance,
A love story written in fate's own chance.

Connected like constellations above,
In the vast expanse, only you I love.
Through galaxies spun by celestial light,
We find our way home, igniting the night.

In this dance of us, eternally bright,
Held close in the dark, two souls in flight.
With every turn, our spirits entwined,
This infinite love, forever unconfined.

Heartbeats Across Eternity

In silence we listen to the gentle thrum,
A cadence of love, where we both come from.
With fingers entwined, we breathe in sync,
Our souls become one, deeper than ink.

Across the ages, our echoes persist,
In every heartbeat, you find me missed.
With rhythm and pulse, we rise and then fall,
In this timeless dance, we hear the call.

Moments cascade like grains of sand,
Each one a treasure, perfectly planned.
Through trials and tears, we weather the storm,
In every heartbeat, our spirits transform.

Time stretches thin, yet love feels so wide,
With you by my side, I always confide.
Together we journey, with hearts unchained,
In the vast temple where love is retained.

With whispers of hope on the wings of fate,
We navigate paths love dares to create.
In the symphony played, we find our song,
Heartbeats across time, where we both belong.

Fusion of Two Souls

In the quiet of night, our spirits collide,
Two flames igniting, where magic won't hide.
With every glance, we spark and ignite,
Creating a fusion, a brilliant light.

Bound by a force that we can't resist,
In your warm embrace, I find my bliss.
Together we merge, like rivers that flow,
A tapestry woven, as time starts to slow.

With laughter and joy, we craft our own space,
In a universe vast, we find our grace.
Our hopes interlace, our dreams intertwine,
Like stars in the night, our paths align.

Through shadows and light, we journey ahead,
In each other's arms, no words need be said.
For in this fusion, we find who we are,
Two souls intertwined, like the moon and star.

Embraced by a love that will never grow old,
In this sacred bond, our story unfolds.
Together forever, no distance can sever,
In the fusion of us, we are one, forever.

Circles of Connection

In the center we stand, two hearts combined,
Drawing circles of love, elegantly aligned.
With each gentle pulse, our spirits unite,
Crafting a bond that feels effortlessly right.

Through twists and turns, we laugh and we cry,
In circles of connection, together we fly.
Embracing the journey, hand in hand we roam,
In each other's light, we find our true home.

With echoes of laughter, the world fades away,
In circles we dance, come what may, we sway.
With whispers of trust, we build our domain,
In this sacred space, we shelter from pain.

In moments of stillness, we share every breath,
Celebrating love that conquers all death.
Every heartbeat a token, a promise so dear,
In these circles we create, we hold each other near.

As constellations twinkle, all stars in a row,
In circles of connection, our love continues to grow.
For in this embrace, we thrive and we shine,
Two souls spinning freely, forever divine.

Milton Keynes UK
Ingram Content Group UK Ltd.
UKHW021001241024
450188UK00012B/519